MIND OVER MATTER

Leading with Trust, Building Positivity,
and Believing in Your Best Future

Winsome Campbell

Copyright © 2024 Winsome Campbell

All rights reserved

The people and events portrayed in this book are fictitious. No real names were mentioned. Any similarity to real persons, living or dead, is coincidental and not intended by the author.

No part of this book may be reproduced, or stored in a retrieval system, or transmitted in any form or by any means, electronic, mechanical, photocopying, recording, or otherwise, without express written permission of the publisher.

Printed in the United States of America

CONTENTS

Title Page
Copyright
Mind Over Matter 1
Introduction 2
Chapter 1: The Power of Perspective 3
Chapter 2: Navigating Jealousy and Negativity 6
Chapter 3: Building Trust, One Step at a Time 13
Chapter 4: The Boss Who Believed in Me 18
Chapter 5: Mastering Communication and Collaboration 23
Chapter 6: Developing a Resilient Mindset 29
Chapter 7: Cultivating Positivity Amidst Challenges 38
Chapter 8: Leadership Through Trust and Empathy 43
Chapter 9: The Journey to Your Best Future 49
Chapter 10: Believe and Achieve 55
About The Author 61

MIND OVER MATTER

*Leading with Trust, Building
Positivity, and Believing
in Your Best Future*

Winsome Campbell

INTRODUCTION

"The journey of a thousand miles begins with a single step."
— *Lao Tzu*

Welcome to *Mind Over Matter*, a guide to transforming your life by mastering your thoughts, fostering trust, and creating positivity in every environment. This book is born from personal experiences, lessons learned, and strategies that will empower you to overcome challenges and embrace a brighter future. Whether you're seeking to enhance your personal relationships, navigate professional dynamics, or develop a stronger sense of self-belief, this book will provide you with the tools and insights you need to make lasting, positive changes in your life.

Through each chapter, you will learn how to harness the power of your mindset, build meaningful connections, and face life's challenges with resilience and optimism. I have walked the path of self-discovery and growth, and I want to share with you the methods and principles that have helped me transform my life. But this is not just a book to read—it's an invitation to embark on a journey with me, step by step, towards creating the life you truly deserve.

So, let's begin this transformational journey together. The first step is simple: believe that you have the power to change, because the mind is powerful beyond measure. And when you master it, you can achieve anything.

CHAPTER 1: THE POWER OF PERSPECTIVE

"Your perspective will either become your prison or your passport." — Steven Furtick

The way we see the world influences everything about our lives. Our perspective is not only shaped by our past experiences, but it also governs how we respond to new challenges, opportunities, and interactions. Mindset is everything. And in this chapter, we will explore how the way you think can profoundly shape your reality.

Your mindset can be compared to a lens through which you view the world. When that lens is clouded by negativity, fear, or self-doubt, your perception becomes skewed, making it harder to see opportunities, solutions, and even your own potential. However, when you adopt a positive and growth-oriented mindset, everything begins to shift.

The science behind perspective is rooted in neuroplasticity—the brain's ability to reorganize itself by forming new neural connections. This means that by consciously choosing to shift our thoughts, we can rewire our brains to think more positively and embrace challenges as opportunities for growth.

In a world full of distractions and pressures, it's easy to fall into patterns of negative thinking. But it's important to recognize that we have the power to break these patterns and reshape the way we approach life. In this chapter, you'll learn how to develop a mindset that sees possibilities instead of roadblocks, solutions instead of problems, and growth instead of failure.

The key to shifting your perspective is to practice awareness. Often, we don't realize the negative self-talk that's running in the background of our minds. But with mindfulness and self-reflection, you can start to identify those thoughts that are limiting your potential. From there, you can begin the process of replacing them with empowering beliefs that will fuel your growth and success.

Here are a few practical exercises to help you change your perspective:

Gratitude: Every morning, write down three things you are grateful for. It can be something as simple as a hot cup of coffee or the support of a friend. By focusing on the positive, you start to see the good in every situation.

When faced with a challenge, ask yourself, "What is the opportunity here?" Reframing allows you to look at difficult situations from a different angle and discover hidden lessons or growth potential.

Be open to visualizing your future: Spend a few minutes each day visualizing your ideal future. Picture yourself succeeding in your goals and living a life aligned with your values. This practice can help you see the possibilities rather than the obstacles.

I remember a time in my own life when everything felt overwhelming. I was stuck in a job that wasn't fulfilling, surrounded by negativity, and struggling to see the way forward. It wasn't until I made the conscious decision to shift my perspective that things started to change. I began by focusing on what I could control—my thoughts. I started practicing gratitude daily and reframing my challenges as opportunities to learn and grow. Slowly but surely, my mindset began to shift, and with it, my reality. I got a clicker watch that helped me keep track of how many times I repeated words of gratitude.

I soon found myself in a career of teaching in the classroom that was aligned with my passions, surrounded by people who supported and encouraged me, and most importantly, I discovered a sense of peace and purpose I had never experienced before. The shift in perspective didn't happen overnight, but it was the catalyst for everything that followed.

Changing your perspective is not just about looking on the bright side—it's about changing the way you approach life. It's about seeing every situation as a chance to learn, grow, and become the person you were meant to be. By shifting your mindset, you unlock a world of new possibilities.

As we continue this journey together, remember that your thoughts shape your reality. Embrace the power of perspective, and you'll begin to see the world in a completely new light. In the next chapter, we'll explore how to navigate jealousy and negativity, so you can maintain your positive mindset and focus on what truly matters.

CHAPTER 2: NAVIGATING JEALOUSY AND NEGATIVITY

"Don't let someone else's opinion of you become your reality." — Les Brown

Jealousy and negativity are powerful emotions that can derail your progress and cloud your judgment. Whether in the workplace, in personal relationships, or within ourselves, these feelings can often hold us back from realizing our potential and achieving our goals. However, understanding how to navigate these emotions and maintain a clear, positive mindset is crucial for both personal and professional growth. In this chapter, we will explore how to rise above jealousy and negativity with grace, self-awareness, and actionable steps that will empower you to maintain focus on your own path.

Jealousy is an emotion that many people experience but rarely talk about. It can arise when you perceive someone else's success or qualities as superior to your own, triggering feelings of inadequacy or envy. Negative thoughts, on the other hand, often occur when we focus on what's wrong in a situation instead of what could go right. Both emotions are rooted in comparison and scarcity—the idea that there's only a limited amount of success or happiness to go around. This is a scarcity and lack mentality that you can replace with an abundance mindset.

While these emotions are natural, they become toxic when they start to consume us, influence our behavior, and limit our ability to think clearly and act confidently. Jealousy can lead to resentment, undermining our relationships and our self-esteem. Negativity can drain our energy, creating a mindset of defeat and hopelessness. But by recognizing and addressing these emotions head-on, we can free ourselves from their grasp and create a space for positivity, growth, and self-empowerment.

Acknowledging and Understanding Jealousy

The first step in managing jealousy is to acknowledge it. Often, people try to ignore or suppress their feelings of envy, thinking they will go away on their own. However, when we suppress emotions like jealousy, they only grow stronger and can manifest in unhealthy ways, such as passive-aggressive behavior or self-sabotage.

Instead of ignoring jealousy, begin by observing it without judgment. Ask yourself, *What is it about this situation or person that's triggering these feelings?* Perhaps you admire their achievements, or maybe their success makes you question your own abilities. By identifying the root cause of your jealousy, you gain insight into what you truly desire and what areas of your life may need attention.

For example, if you feel jealous of a coworker's promotion, take a moment to reflect on why you feel this way. Are you frustrated with your own career progression? Do you feel unappreciated or overlooked? By pinpointing the underlying cause of your jealousy, you can begin to shift your focus from comparison to self-improvement.

Transforming Negativity into Opportunity

Negativity often arises from focusing too much on what's going wrong instead of what's going right. It's easy to become overwhelmed by problems, especially when things aren't going the way you want them to. But the key to overcoming negativity is shifting your mindset from a problem-focused perspective to a solution-oriented one.

When you find yourself slipping into negative thinking, try to pause and ask yourself, *What can I learn from this situation?* This simple question can change your outlook entirely. Rather than ruminating on the things you can't control, focus on what you can do to move forward. By reframing the situation in terms of growth and opportunity, you begin to reclaim your power and positivity.

Practical Steps to Overcome Jealousy and Negativity

Here are several practical steps you can take to rise above jealousy and negativity:

1. **Practice Gratitude**: One of the most effective ways to combat jealousy and negativity is through gratitude. By focusing on the things you are grateful for in your life, you shift your attention from scarcity to abundance. When you feel envious of someone else, remind yourself of your own unique strengths and accomplishments. Write down three things you're grateful for every day to help shift your mindset.
2. **Reframe Your Thoughts**: As mentioned earlier, reframing is a powerful technique for transforming negative thoughts. Instead of thinking, *Why did they get the promotion and not me?* reframe the thought to, *What can I learn from this person's success?* By focusing on learning and growth, you can turn jealousy into inspiration.
3. **Focus on Your Own Journey**: It's easy to get caught up in what others are doing, especially with social media constantly showcasing the best moments of everyone's lives. But remember, comparison is the

thief of joy. Keep your focus on your own goals and progress. Every step you take toward your dreams is a victory, no matter how small.
4. **Surround Yourself with Positivity**: The people you surround yourself with have a huge impact on your mindset. If you find that certain individuals or environments trigger negative emotions, consider how you can limit your exposure to them or set boundaries. Seek out relationships with people who uplift, support, and encourage you to be your best self.
5. **Invest in Self-Improvement**: If jealousy is stemming from a perceived lack in your own abilities, take it as an opportunity to invest in your personal growth. Whether it's taking a course, reading books, or working with a mentor, investing in yourself is the best way to combat feelings of inadequacy.

True story

When I first started at my job, I was excited and eager to make a positive impression. I prided myself on being welcoming and open, treating everyone with kindness, no matter their position. One of those individuals was a new colleague who had started working at the same time as me. I made sure to greet her warmly and offered assistance when needed. After all, I believe in creating a positive work environment by connecting with everyone I come across. We didn't interact much at first, but when I found myself balancing my teaching job with a part-time position, I started noticing her more.

My part-time job wasn't far from my primary teaching role, just three minutes away by Uber. However, I was having some car trouble at the time and had to rely on ridesharing. Since it was only a few minutes from work, I didn't mind the quick trip. One day, she offered to take me to my part-time job. Though I wasn't particularly comfortable accepting the offer, I reluctantly canceled my Uber and accepted her kind gesture. It wasn't something I wanted to do, but I thought, "Why not?" at the time. After that, we didn't run into each other much outside of work-related tasks.

Over the next few months, we exchanged casual conversations, but something felt off. As time passed, I started to notice a shift in her behavior. She seemed to gossip about others at work in a way that didn't sit right with me. I've always believed in maintaining professionalism, and I quickly found myself questioning the direction of these conversations. I didn't want to get caught up in workplace drama, so I chose to set boundaries and keep things at arm's length.

To my surprise, she started distancing herself from me. She would stare at me for long, uncomfortable moments. It was unsettling, especially considering how I'd always been cordial and professional. There was a period when she would greet me with an overly cheerful "Good morning!" as she passed me to enter a professional space we all used. It felt almost forced, like she was trying to prove something. But after a while, even that stopped. She stopped greeting me altogether, which was strange considering the initial warmth. I continued to focus on my work, ignoring the odd change in behavior.

As weeks went by, I noticed how she would often try to draw me into uncomfortable conversations. She'd ask questions like, "Did you buy a car?" or "Why do you come to work so early?" Her tone was always negative and critical, and I could tell she was trying to provoke a reaction. It was clear that her questions were not out of genuine curiosity but rather an attempt to rattle me. I found the way she spoke to me insulting and dismissive. I didn't feel the need to answer her questions in any meaningful way because it seemed like an attempt to create tension.

She even seemed to want a confrontation, but I wasn't going to give her the satisfaction. Instead of engaging in her provocations, I chose to maintain my professionalism. I didn't answer her directly and instead kept my responses minimal. Eventually, I began to forget she even worked there, as I was so focused on my own tasks and responsibilities.

It was puzzling when I later found out that she went to our boss to complain about me. To my knowledge, I had never had any negative interactions with her or anyone else at work. I always kept my focus on my role and stayed out of unnecessary conflict. It was clear to me that she was not handling the situation professionally. I remained calm, knowing that I had nothing to hide and had done nothing to warrant a complaint. My boss had always been supportive of my work and my achievements, which reinforced my confidence in my actions.

The entire situation seemed like a classic case of jealousy. She didn't seem to understand the concept of minding your own business and focusing on your personal goals. It became evident that her discomfort with me wasn't rooted in anything I had done wrong, but rather in her own insecurities and perhaps envy of my work ethic, my position, and the way I carried myself. I didn't feel the need to explain myself to her, and I didn't entertain the idea of engaging in her negativity.

To me, this experience became an opportunity to practice what I preach—mastering my thoughts and focusing on overcoming my own challenges. I wasn't going to let her attempt to stir up drama affect me or my performance. I chose to remain calm and professional, handling the situation with grace. It's a mindset that's served me well throughout my life—focus on what you can control, don't engage in drama, and rise above negativity.

In the end, I learned an important lesson about how people's actions often have little to do with you and everything to do with them. Her behavior wasn't about me; it was about her own struggles. And while I couldn't control her actions, I could control how I responded. I chose to stay true to myself and my values, knowing that I was in the right. And in the end, I didn't let her negativity impact my journey. I continued to stay focused on my role, my tasks, and my growth—because, at the end of the day, it's all about mastering your own mind and staying true to your path.

Jealousy and negativity are natural emotions, but they don't have to control your life. By acknowledging these feelings, understanding their root causes, and taking proactive steps to overcome them, you can reclaim your energy and focus on what truly matters—your own personal growth and happiness. The journey to positivity begins with the decision to rise above comparison and negativity. In the next chapter, we'll explore how building trust, both with others and yourself, is essential for creating healthy relationships and achieving your goals.

CHAPTER 3: BUILDING TRUST, ONE STEP AT A TIME

"Trust is built with consistency." — Lincoln Chafee

Trust is the foundation of every meaningful relationship, whether personal, professional, or even the relationship you have with yourself. Without trust, communication falters, collaboration struggles, and opportunities for growth are lost. In this chapter, we'll delve into the principles of building trust with others and, perhaps more importantly, with yourself. We'll explore how trust is not a one-time event, but a process—a series of steps that, when taken consistently, lead to stronger bonds and a more empowered, resilient self.

Trust is the cornerstone of all human connections. When you trust someone, you open yourself up to vulnerability, knowing that the other person will honor your feelings, thoughts, and intentions. In professional settings, trust facilitates collaboration and innovation, allowing teams to function smoothly and achieve shared goals. In personal relationships, trust fosters intimacy and emotional support, making it possible to face life's challenges together.

However, trust is fragile. It can be broken in an instant by betrayal, dishonesty, or inconsistency. While rebuilding trust is possible, it requires time, effort, and a commitment to transparency and integrity. That's why it's crucial to build trust from the start—strong and steady, one step at a time.

Building trust with others is a gradual process, requiring consistency, reliability, and clear communication. Whether you're working with colleagues, making new friends, or trying to strengthen your existing relationships, the way you interact with people plays a significant role in how much they trust you.

One of the most important ways to build trust is by being reliable. People need to know that they can count on you, whether it's for small tasks or significant responsibilities. If you consistently follow through on your commitments, others will see you as someone who can be trusted.

In professional environments, being reliable means meeting deadlines, delivering quality work, and supporting your team when needed. In personal relationships, it means being there for someone when you say you will be, showing up when you're expected, and honoring your promises.

Clear, honest communication is key to building trust. When you communicate openly, you reduce the chances of misunderstandings and foster an environment of transparency. If something goes wrong or if there's an issue, address it head-on. Don't let problems fester or hide behind silence.

One example of effective communication is admitting when you don't know something or when you've made a mistake. Acknowledging your shortcomings demonstrates humility and helps others see that you're open to growth and improvement. People trust those who are willing to be vulnerable and honest about their experiences.

Consistency in your actions and behavior is another critical element in building trust. If your actions match your words, people will begin to trust you. However, inconsistency creates doubt and uncertainty, which can erode trust over time.

To build consistency, make sure that you are aligned with your values and principles. When your behavior is predictable and dependable, others will feel safe relying on you. Whether you're at work or in a personal relationship, consistency in how you show up builds the foundation for lasting trust.

Trust is not just about reliability; it's also about showing empathy and understanding for others' feelings, needs, and perspectives. When you actively listen to someone, acknowledge their concerns, and show that you care about their well-being, trust flourishes. People trust those who make them feel heard, respected, and valued.

Empathy requires being present in the moment, offering support, and showing kindness, even when the other person's feelings may seem difficult to understand. Empathy strengthens relationships because it establishes a deep emotional connection that goes beyond words or actions.

Building trust with others is undoubtedly important, but the most critical relationship you will ever have is the one with yourself. If you don't trust yourself, it becomes difficult to make decisions, follow through on commitments, and believe in your own abilities. Trusting yourself means having confidence in your judgment, aligning your actions with your values, and believing that you can handle whatever life throws your way.

One of the most effective ways to build trust with yourself is by honoring your word. If you tell yourself that you're going to do something—whether it's waking up early to exercise or completing a project on time—make sure you follow through. Every time you fail to keep your commitments to yourself, you erode your sense of self-trust.

On the other hand, when you honor your promises, you reinforce your belief in your own abilities. You begin to see yourself as someone who is reliable, dependable, and capable of achieving your goals.

Another way to build self-trust is through self-compassion. We all make mistakes, but it's how we respond to those mistakes that shapes our relationship with ourselves. When you make an error or face failure, instead of criticizing yourself harshly, offer yourself the same understanding and kindness you would offer to a friend.

Self-compassion creates an environment of growth, allowing you to learn from your mistakes rather than being paralyzed by them. When you treat yourself with kindness, you start to trust that you'll recover and improve, no matter what challenges you face.

Building trust with yourself also means setting boundaries. If you say yes to everything and everyone, you risk depleting your energy and losing sight of your own needs and desires. Setting healthy boundaries allows you to honor your values, protect your time, and ensure that you're living in alignment with your goals.

Trust yourself enough to say no when necessary. Trust that you have the strength and wisdom to prioritize your well-being. When you set boundaries, you are demonstrating to yourself that you can be trusted to make decisions that support your happiness and growth.

Trust as a Lifelong Journey

Building trust with others and with yourself is not something that happens overnight. It's a lifelong journey that requires patience, practice, and persistence. Trust takes time to develop, and once broken, it can take even longer to rebuild. However, by being reliable, honest, consistent, and empathetic, you can create a strong foundation of trust that will serve you in all areas of your life.

As you continue to foster trust with yourself and others, remember that every step you take strengthens your ability to face challenges, build relationships, and achieve your goals. In the next chapter, we'll dive into the impact of mentorship and support, drawing from my own personal story of a boss who believed in me when I needed it most.

CHAPTER 4: THE BOSS WHO BELIEVED IN ME

"A good leader inspires people to have confidence in the leader; a great leader inspires people to have confidence in themselves." — Eleanor Roosevelt

Sometimes, support comes from unexpected places. In the most unlikely of circumstances, someone can believe in you when you might not even believe in yourself. That's what happened to me in my early career, and it marked a pivotal turning point in my professional journey. This chapter tells the story of how one boss's unwavering belief in me reshaped my perception of my potential and opened doors to opportunities I hadn't even considered. It's a story of mentorship, encouragement, and the transformative power of someone seeing something in you that you couldn't see at the time.

When I started my career, I was filled with ambition but also a deep sense of insecurity. I had big dreams and the drive to succeed, but I often found myself doubting whether I was truly capable of achieving those dreams. In meetings, I'd second-guess my ideas, constantly measuring my contributions against the more experienced colleagues around me. I was eager to learn, but I didn't yet have the confidence to trust my instincts.

In those early days, it felt like the only thing standing between me and success was my own self-doubt. While I tried my best to stay focused and work hard, there was always that lingering feeling of uncertainty. I often found myself stuck in a cycle of striving for approval, seeking validation from others to reassure myself that I was on the right path. I needed a break—a moment where someone would believe in me, even if I didn't believe in myself.

Enter My Boss: A Turning Point

That's when I met my boss. She was the kind of leader who could see past surface-level performances and understood the potential that often hides behind a layer of self-doubt. She was a mentor in every sense of the word—someone who didn't just manage the team but actively invested in helping each individual grow and reach their full potential.

When I first started working in my workplace I expected nothing more than a professional relationship where I would learn the ropes and contribute where needed. But she had different plans. From day one, she saw something in me that I couldn't see in myself: the capacity to take on bigger challenges and push beyond the limits I had set for myself as an Educator. Her belief in me was not only empowering—it was life-changing.

She didn't just offer praise for the work I was doing; she challenged me. She would give me goals that seemed daunting and outside my comfort zone. At first, I was hesitant, questioning whether I was truly capable. But she would consistently offer support and guidance, always reinforcing the idea that I had the skills to succeed, even when I wasn't sure. "You're dedicated, passionate and growing in your practice," she'd say. "Trust yourself, and I trust you."

Her belief in me was like a mirror, reflecting my potential when I couldn't see it myself. She taught me the value of stepping outside my comfort zone and taking risks. I began to trust her judgment and, slowly, my own. Each tasks I successfully completed under her mentorship built my confidence and reaffirmed the idea that maybe I *was* capable of more than I had initially believed.

The Power of Mentorship

Her mentorship wasn't just about providing guidance on tasks and assignments—it was about fostering an environment where I could thrive. She took the time to understand my strengths and weaknesses and provided constructive feedback that helped me grow. But what stood out the most was her ability to empower me to make decisions on my own, encouraging independence while also offering support when I needed it.

Mentorship is a powerful tool for growth, and she embodied the qualities of an ideal mentor. She didn't micromanage, but she always offered great tips that I could use to leverage the success I had achieved with the classes. She didn't just point out what I could improve but also celebrated my successes, big and small. With her encouragement, I started to see that I was capable of handling more responsibility and that my voice was valuable in meetings and decision-making processes.

Her belief in me didn't stop at the work I was doing. She took a genuine interest in my career goals and personal development, offering advice on how to navigate the company and advance in my career. She often spoke about leadership, not just as a position of authority, but as a role that required empathy, integrity, and trust. Through her, I learned that leadership wasn't about having all the answers but about creating an environment where people felt safe to grow and contribute.

Overcoming Challenges Together

There were times when I faced challenges that made me question everything I was learning. There were goals that didn't go as planned, deadlines that were missed, and moments when I felt like I had failed. Each time I hit a roadblock, she was there to offer perspective and encouragement. She didn't see setbacks as failures but as opportunities to learn and grow. She taught me that mistakes were a natural part of the journey and that the key to success was not avoiding mistakes but embracing them as part of the learning process.

There was a time when I had a difficult class. It seemed I was not making an impact. But instead of allowing me to give in to frustration, she encouraged me to approach the situation with a calm, strategic mindset. I didn't focus on how hard it seemed at the time. Instead I focus on the small steps I could take to keep moving forward in my practice. What I learnt from all that is I didn't have to solve everything at once and that success was built one step at a time.

With her support, I was able to pull the the semesters together, and it ended up being one of the most successful school year I had led. The experience taught me valuable lessons about leadership, problem-solving, and resilience. It also solidified my trust in God and her guidance and reinforced the importance of having a mentor who believes in you, especially during times of doubt.

The Impact of Belief

What my boss did for me was more than just offering guidance or advice. She gave me something far more powerful: belief. Belief in my potential, belief in my ability to learn and grow, and belief that I could handle whatever challenges came my way. Her support gave me the confidence to step into roles I never thought I could fill and to take on responsibilities I once thought were out of my reach.

Looking back, I realize that belief is one of the most powerful tools for personal and professional growth. When someone believes in you, it not only motivates you to work harder but also encourages you to trust yourself more. The belief that others have in us can act as a mirror, reflecting back our capabilities when we doubt them. But perhaps even more importantly, it teaches us how to believe in ourselves.

The lessons I learned from my boss continue to shape my career and my life. Now, as a mentor myself, I strive to pay forward the belief and encouragement she gave me. I understand the impact that a single person's belief can have on someone's journey, and I am committed to fostering an environment where others feel supported and empowered to reach their potential.

If there's one thing I've learned from my experience with my boss, it's that mentorship isn't just about teaching skills—it's about inspiring belief. When we believe in others, we help them see what they are capable of, often before they see it themselves. And in doing so, we create a ripple effect of growth, confidence, and success.

CHAPTER 5: MASTERING COMMUNICATION AND COLLABORATION

"The single biggest problem in communication is the illusion that it has taken place." — George Bernard Shaw

Effective communication is one of the most crucial skills for success in both personal and professional environments. The way we convey our thoughts, ideas, and emotions can make or break relationships, impact our career trajectories, and shape the culture of our teams and organizations. However, mastering communication is not just about how well we express ourselves, but also about how we listen, collaborate, and adapt our approach to different contexts and people. In this chapter, we will explore strategies for enhancing your communication skills, fostering collaboration, and creating harmonious relationships that can propel you forward in life.

The Foundation of Effective Communication

Before we dive into the specifics of mastering communication, it's essential to understand the foundation of effective communication itself. At its core, communication is the exchange of information, thoughts, and feelings between individuals. But successful communication involves much more than merely sending and receiving messages—it requires clarity, empathy, and active listening.

The first step toward mastering communication is to be mindful of how you convey your thoughts. Words matter, but how you say them—your tone, body language, and facial expressions—can speak volumes. Misunderstandings often arise not from what is being said, but from how it is interpreted. This is where emotional intelligence (EI) plays a vital role.

Emotional Intelligence in Communication: Emotional intelligence is the ability to recognize, understand, and manage our own emotions and those of others. When we are emotionally intelligent, we can navigate difficult conversations with empathy, manage our reactions in tense situations, and communicate in ways that foster connection rather than conflict. High EI allows us to read nonverbal cues, understand how our words affect others, and adjust our approach to ensure that we're being understood in the way we intend.

The Importance of Active Listening

Communication isn't a one-way street—it's an interactive process. While speaking clearly is crucial, listening actively is just as important. Active listening means paying full attention to the speaker, understanding their message, responding thoughtfully, and remembering what was said. This is often easier said than done, especially in today's world, where distractions abound.

Listening actively helps us gain a deeper understanding of the person we're communicating with and shows that we respect their point of view. It's a key element of building trust and rapport. When we listen attentively, we're more likely to respond in ways that acknowledge the other person's perspective, which can defuse potential misunderstandings and create a sense of mutual respect.

One way to improve your listening skills is to practice "reflective listening." This technique involves paraphrasing what the other person has said to ensure you've understood their message correctly. For example, if a colleague expresses frustration with a project, you might say, "It sounds like you're feeling overwhelmed by the workload and need more support. Is that right?" This approach not only clarifies your understanding but also validates the other person's feelings.

Trust is the cornerstone of any healthy relationship, whether it's personal, professional, or within a team. And communication is the key to building and maintaining that trust. When we communicate openly and honestly, we show that we can be relied upon to share information accurately and in a timely manner. On the other hand, poor communication—whether through withholding information, being vague, or misrepresenting facts—can erode trust and damage relationships.

To build trust, it's important to be transparent in your communication. This doesn't mean sharing every detail of your personal life, but it does mean being open about your thoughts, intentions, and the reasons behind your decisions. When people feel like they can trust you to be truthful and straightforward, they are more likely to feel comfortable collaborating with you and sharing their own thoughts and ideas.

Another way to build trust is through consistency. When you consistently communicate in a clear and respectful manner, others come to know what to expect from you, which helps them feel secure in the relationship. Consistent communication is especially important in team settings, where everyone needs to be aligned on goals, responsibilities, and expectations.

Effective communication is not just about speaking and listening—it's also about collaboration. Collaboration involves working with others to achieve a common goal, and successful collaboration depends on clear, open communication, as well as the ability to navigate differences and leverage diverse perspectives.

One of the most powerful aspects of collaboration is the opportunity to work with people from different backgrounds, experiences, and viewpoints. A diverse team can offer a wealth of ideas and solutions that you may not have considered on your own. However, in order to harness the power of diversity, communication must be inclusive. This means being open to others' ideas, being respectful of differing opinions, and actively encouraging everyone to contribute.

When collaborating, it's essential to create an environment where everyone feels comfortable sharing their thoughts without fear of judgment or dismissal. This can be achieved through practices like active listening, providing constructive feedback, and ensuring that everyone has an equal opportunity to speak. When everyone feels heard, collaboration thrives, and the team can achieve much more than any individual could alone.

In any collaboration, conflict is inevitable. Differences in opinion, misunderstandings, or disagreements are a natural part of working with others. However, how we handle conflict can significantly impact the success of our communication and collaboration efforts.

Rather than avoiding conflict, it's important to approach it with a mindset of empathy and understanding. When conflicts arise, take the time to listen to the other person's perspective and express your own feelings in a respectful, non-confrontational way. Use "I" statements to express your feelings without placing blame, such as "I felt frustrated when…" instead of "You always…" This helps to prevent the other person from becoming defensive and opens the door for productive dialogue.

Another key aspect of resolving conflict is finding common

ground. Instead of focusing solely on the points of disagreement, look for areas where you both agree. This can help to create a sense of unity and collaboration, even in the midst of conflict. Once common ground is established, you can work together to find a solution that meets both of your needs.

As we've discussed, communication is not just about conveying information—it's about doing so in a way that resonates with your audience. Whether you're speaking to a colleague, a client, or a group of stakeholders, it's important to tailor your communication to the context and the individuals involved.

One of the hallmarks of effective communicators is their ability to adapt their communication style to suit different situations. This means being able to adjust your tone, body language, and approach depending on who you're speaking to and the circumstances at hand. For example, you might communicate differently with a close colleague than with a senior executive. Understanding the needs and preferences of your audience allows you to communicate more effectively and increase the impact of your message.

Effective communicators also know how to be concise and clear. In a world where people are constantly bombarded with information, getting to the point quickly and succinctly is crucial. Avoiding jargon, being specific, and using simple language can help ensure that your message is understood and remembered.

Mastering communication and collaboration is an ongoing process—one that requires practice, self-awareness, and a willingness to adapt. By developing these skills, you can build stronger relationships, navigate challenges with greater ease, and create a positive, productive environment for yourself and those around you. Whether you're working in a team, leading a project, or simply interacting with others on a daily basis, the ability to communicate effectively and collaborate with others is key to achieving your goals and fostering success.

As you continue on your journey, remember that communication is not just about talking; it's about connecting. And the more you invest in mastering this skill, the more meaningful and impactful your relationships will become.

CHAPTER 6: DEVELOPING A RESILIENT MINDSET

"It's not whether you get knocked down, it's whether you get up." — Vince Lombardi

Life is filled with ups and downs, challenges and setbacks, but the ability to bounce back stronger from adversity is what truly defines success. Resilience isn't just about surviving tough times—it's about thriving through them and using difficulties as opportunities for growth. Developing a resilient mindset is essential not only for overcoming obstacles but for living a fulfilling, purposeful life. In this chapter, we will explore how to cultivate resilience in your mindset, how to stay strong in the face of adversity, and the strategies that can help you bounce back from setbacks with renewed determination.

Resilience is often misunderstood as the ability to "tough it out" or endure hardship without breaking. While it does involve strength, resilience is much more than simply enduring. It's about flexibility, adaptability, and perseverance. Resilience involves maintaining a positive outlook, learning from failures, and adjusting your approach in the face of challenges.

One of the key elements of resilience is the ability to recover from setbacks. Life doesn't always go according to plan—whether it's a career setback, a personal loss, or a difficult situation—it's how we respond to these challenges that matters. Resilient individuals don't avoid adversity; they face it head-on with a sense of agency, knowing that they can learn from their experiences and grow stronger as a result.

A key aspect of developing resilience is the ability to shift your perspective. When things go wrong, it's easy to fall into a victim mindset and believe that the world is against you. But a resilient mindset reframes adversity as an opportunity to learn, grow, and improve.

The concept of a growth mindset, popularized by psychologist Carol Dweck, is central to resilience. People with a growth mindset believe that their abilities and intelligence are not fixed; they can develop and improve through effort and perseverance. When faced with a challenge, they don't see it as a reflection of their limitations but as a stepping stone toward growth.

For example, instead of seeing a failure as an end point, someone with a growth mindset would view it as a valuable learning experience. They might ask themselves, "What can I learn from this?" or "How can I approach this differently next time?" This shift in thinking helps to maintain motivation and momentum, even in difficult times.

Developing Emotional Agility

One of the most important aspects of resilience is emotional agility—the ability to process and respond to your emotions in a healthy, constructive way. It's normal to feel frustrated, sad, or angry when faced with adversity, but how you handle those emotions can make all the difference in your resilience.

Emotional regulation is the ability to manage your emotional responses, especially in challenging or stressful situations. This doesn't mean suppressing your emotions or pretending everything is okay when it's not. Instead, it's about acknowledging your feelings, allowing yourself to experience them fully, and then choosing how to respond.

When faced with a setback, a resilient person might feel upset or discouraged but doesn't allow those emotions to take over. Instead, they might practice mindfulness or deep breathing to center themselves, process their emotions, and regain focus. This helps to avoid being overwhelmed by negative emotions and enables them to approach the situation with a clear mind.

Another critical component of emotional agility is self-compassion. Resilient individuals show kindness and understanding to themselves, even when they make mistakes or face difficulties. Rather than being overly self-critical, they treat themselves with the same care and compassion they would offer a friend.

When you practice self-compassion, you allow yourself to be imperfect. You acknowledge that setbacks and failures are part of the human experience, and you give yourself permission to try again. This mindset encourages persistence and keeps you moving forward, even when the path seems difficult.

While resilience is often thought of as an individual trait, it is equally important to have a strong support network to help you through challenging times. Resilient people understand that they don't have to face adversity alone. They reach out to others for support, guidance, and encouragement when needed.

A strong support network provides emotional stability, practical advice, and a sense of belonging. Whether it's family, friends, colleagues, or mentors, having people to turn to can make all the difference when things get tough. Studies have shown that people who have strong social connections are better able to cope with stress, recover from illness, and navigate life's challenges.

It's important to cultivate relationships with people who are positive, supportive, and uplifting. Surrounding yourself with individuals who encourage you and believe in your potential can help you maintain hope and motivation, even in difficult times. These relationships provide a safe space for expressing your emotions, gaining perspective, and receiving feedback.

Having a sense of purpose is one of the most powerful ways to cultivate resilience. When you have a clear vision of what you're working toward, it becomes easier to persevere through challenges. Purpose gives you the strength to keep going, even when things aren't going as planned.

To develop a resilient mindset, it's important to connect with your "why"—the deeper reasons behind your goals and actions. Ask yourself: Why do you do what you do? What motivates you to keep going, even when the road gets tough? When you have a clear sense of purpose, setbacks feel less like obstacles and more like temporary challenges to overcome on the path to your greater goal.

Purpose also gives you direction. When life throws you off course, having a strong sense of purpose can help you realign and refocus. It serves as a compass, guiding you through uncertain times and reminding you of the bigger picture.

Resilience is not a passive trait. It requires action—sometimes small, consistent actions and sometimes bold, courageous steps. Resilient people don't just wait for things to get better; they take proactive steps to move forward, even when they're unsure of the outcome.

One way to build resilience through action is to focus on small wins. When facing a large challenge, it can be overwhelming to think about the long road ahead. But breaking down the task into smaller, manageable steps allows you to make progress, no matter how small. Each small win boosts your confidence and reinforces the belief that you can overcome any obstacle.

Resilience also involves the willingness to take calculated risks and step outside your comfort zone. It's easy to stay safe and avoid challenges, but growth happens when you stretch yourself. Resilient individuals aren't afraid to fail because they understand that failure is often a stepping stone to success.

Developing a resilient mindset is not about avoiding adversity—it's about learning how to handle life's challenges with grace, strength, and perseverance. It's about shifting your perspective, processing your emotions in a healthy way, building supportive relationships, and taking proactive steps to move forward. Resilience is a skill that can be cultivated through practice, and it is one of the most powerful tools you can possess in your journey toward personal and professional fulfillment.

Remember, resilience doesn't mean you won't experience difficulties—it means you have the inner strength to navigate them and come out stronger on the other side. Keep building your resilience, and you'll find that no matter what life throws your way, you have the power to overcome it and continue moving toward your best future.

Self-reflection is an essential tool in developing resilience because it allows you to process experiences, learn from them, and adjust your approach for the future. After facing adversity, take the time to reflect on what happened, how you reacted, and what you might do differently next time. This practice helps you gain insight into your own thought patterns and behaviors, empowering you to make better decisions moving forward.

One of the most effective ways to engage in self-reflection is through journaling. Writing down your thoughts, feelings, and reactions to challenges can provide clarity and help you understand your emotional triggers. Journaling allows you to step back from the situation and assess it from a more objective point of view. It can also serve as a record of your progress, showing you how much you've grown over time.

Take a moment to ask yourself reflective questions after a setback. For example:

- What was the lesson in this experience?
- How did I handle my emotions, and could I have done so differently?
- What strengths did I draw on during this challenge?
- What could I have done to prepare better or manage the situation differently?

Through regular self-reflection, you begin to see patterns in your responses to adversity, which helps you develop healthier strategies for dealing with similar challenges in the future.

Mindfulness is a powerful practice that can enhance your resilience by grounding you in the present moment and helping you manage stress. When faced with difficulties, it's easy to become overwhelmed by the "what-ifs" and the fear of failure. Mindfulness teaches you to focus on the here and now, rather than getting lost in hypothetical outcomes.

Simple mindfulness exercises like deep breathing, body scans, and meditation can help you maintain emotional balance in stressful situations. These practices allow you to acknowledge your emotions without letting them control you. By staying present, you can better regulate your stress response and think more clearly about the next steps to take.

Incorporating mindfulness into your daily routine helps you develop resilience over time. It teaches you to respond to challenges with awareness and calmness rather than reacting impulsively. As you practice mindfulness, you'll find that you can face difficulties with more clarity and less emotional reactivity, ultimately boosting your capacity to handle adversity.

Physical health plays a crucial role in mental resilience. When you take care of your body, you provide a solid foundation for handling stress and overcoming challenges. Exercise, nutrition, and sleep all influence your emotional well-being and ability to cope with difficulties.

Regular physical activity helps reduce stress and anxiety, boosts mood, and increases energy levels. Exercise also helps regulate the body's stress response, making it easier to maintain focus and clarity when facing adversity. Whether it's a morning jog, a yoga session, or a simple walk around the block, movement is a powerful way to strengthen both your physical and mental resilience.

Sleep is another critical factor in building resilience. Adequate rest is essential for emotional regulation, decision-making, and cognitive function. When you're well-rested, you are better able to respond to challenges with patience and clarity. Lack of sleep, on the other hand, can make you more irritable and less able to cope with stress. Prioritizing sleep is an often-overlooked aspect of resilience, but it plays a vital role in your ability to stay grounded during tough times.

A healthy diet fuels both your body and mind. Proper nutrition helps stabilize mood, reduce anxiety, and improve focus. Eating a balanced diet rich in nutrients provides the energy you need to stay resilient, even when life gets tough. It's important to stay hydrated and avoid excessive consumption of caffeine or sugar, which can lead to mood swings and energy crashes.

By integrating these habits into your routine, you create a strong foundation for mental resilience. Taking care of your body enables you to stay focused, energized, and capable of managing challenges with greater ease.

Resilience is not only important in your personal life but also in your professional life. Workplaces can be demanding and high-pressure environments, and it's easy to become overwhelmed by deadlines, expectations, and interpersonal dynamics. Developing resilience at work enables you to remain effective, productive, and positive, even in the face of challenges.

When work becomes overwhelming, it's crucial to take a step back and evaluate the situation. Break large tasks into smaller, more manageable steps, and focus on what you can control. Reach out for help or delegate tasks when needed. By managing your stress effectively, you can prevent burnout and maintain resilience in your professional life.

Another important aspect of workplace resilience is setting boundaries. In today's fast-paced work culture, it's easy to overcommit and spread yourself too thin. Learning to say no, delegate responsibilities, and prioritize self-care can help you maintain resilience and avoid burnout. Setting boundaries allows you to protect your time and energy, ensuring that you can show up as your best self in both your personal and professional life.

One of the greatest benefits of developing resilience is the ability to turn setbacks into opportunities for growth. When you have a resilient mindset, failure doesn't feel like a permanent defeat; it's simply a stepping stone to success. Each challenge you face offers valuable lessons that can help you improve and refine your approach.

By reframing setbacks as opportunities for learning, you can maintain a positive outlook even in the most difficult times. For example, if you face a career setback, rather than seeing it as a failure, you can use it as an opportunity to reassess your skills, reflect on what you could have done differently, and make adjustments for future success. This mindset shift allows you to stay focused on growth rather than being discouraged by temporary obstacles.

Developing resilience is not something that happens overnight. It is a continuous journey, a practice that you build over time. By shifting your perspective, developing emotional agility, building a support network, and practicing mindfulness, you can strengthen your resilience and navigate life's challenges with grace and determination.

Remember, resilience is about bouncing back from setbacks, not avoiding them. It's about learning from adversity, growing stronger through the process, and becoming more capable of handling whatever life throws your way. With each challenge you face, you have the opportunity to develop more resilience and continue moving forward toward your best future. Keep building your resilience, and you will discover that you are far more capable than you ever imagined.

CHAPTER 7: CULTIVATING POSITIVITY AMIDST CHALLENGES

"In the middle of difficulty lies opportunity." — Albert Einstein

Positivity is often mistaken for the absence of difficulties, but in reality, it's about how we respond to challenges. It's the ability to face life's obstacles with optimism, believing that good can emerge from even the toughest circumstances. This chapter explores how to cultivate a positive mindset even when things seem bleak and how positivity can be a transformative tool in both personal and professional settings.

Optimism is more than just thinking happy thoughts; it's a mindset that influences how you perceive and respond to events. A positive mindset doesn't mean you ignore the difficulties or pretend everything is perfect. Instead, it's about choosing to focus on potential solutions and opportunities, even in the midst of adversity. Optimism is the belief that you have the ability to overcome challenges and that setbacks are temporary.

Research has shown that optimism is linked to better health outcomes, higher levels of success, and greater resilience. Studies have found that optimistic people tend to have stronger immune systems, lower levels of stress, and a higher likelihood of achieving their goals. When you cultivate positivity, you are not only improving your emotional well-being but also enhancing your physical health and long-term success.

Positivity allows you to reframe difficult situations. For example, if you lose a job, instead of focusing solely on the disappointment, you can choose to view the situation as an opportunity to pursue something better. The ability to see setbacks as stepping stones is a hallmark of a positive mindset.

A key element of positivity is reframing: changing the way you look at a situation to find the opportunity in it. When faced with challenges, the way you perceive the situation can make all the difference. Instead of dwelling on the negative aspects, you can ask yourself questions that prompt a more optimistic view, such as:

- What can I learn from this situation?
- How can this challenge help me grow as a person?
- What are the potential opportunities here that I haven't seen yet?

Reframing doesn't deny the difficulty of a situation but shifts your focus to what's within your control. This mindset allows you to see problems as opportunities for growth, learning, and transformation.

For instance, if you face a setback in a project or career, instead of thinking, *"I've failed, and it's over,"* you can reframe it as, *"This didn't work out as planned, but it's an opportunity to refine my approach and try again."* By doing so, you embrace the challenge and take proactive steps toward finding a solution.

In the workplace, cultivating positivity is crucial not only for your own well-being but also for creating a productive and harmonious environment. Positive employees are more likely to collaborate, solve problems creatively, and engage with their work. Creating a positive atmosphere at work doesn't mean ignoring difficulties; it means addressing challenges with a constructive, solution-oriented mindset.

One way to cultivate positivity at work is by supporting your colleagues and creating a culture of mutual respect and encouragement. Celebrate small wins, offer words of encouragement, and recognize the efforts of others. When you foster an environment where people feel valued and supported, it becomes easier to navigate tough times as a team.

A positive work culture can reduce stress and increase job satisfaction, which leads to higher levels of motivation and productivity. Even when challenges arise, a positive workplace creates a sense of camaraderie that can help employees bounce back from setbacks faster and with more resilience.

In stressful work situations, maintaining a positive attitude is especially important. When deadlines loom or pressure mounts, it's easy to become overwhelmed. Instead of succumbing to stress, try to break the problem down into smaller tasks and focus on what you can control. Remind yourself of past successes and how you've overcome challenges before. By staying calm and focused, you inspire others to do the same, which helps everyone perform at their best.

Positivity is also essential in personal relationships, whether with family, friends, or romantic partners. When facing conflicts or challenges in relationships, your mindset can influence how you communicate and resolve issues. A positive mindset in relationships means being solution-focused and open to understanding each other's perspectives, rather than dwelling on the problem or assigning blame.

A key element of positivity in relationships is the ability to communicate constructively. When disagreements arise, instead of focusing on negativity or attacking each other, try to engage in open, honest conversations with an emphasis on finding common ground. Positive communication involves active listening, empathy, and understanding. Rather than viewing disagreements as threats, see them as opportunities for growth and deeper connection.

For example, if there's tension in a relationship, approach the conversation with the mindset of *"I want to understand your point of view, and together, we'll find a solution."* This approach fosters cooperation and trust, helping to maintain a positive relationship even in challenging times.

Positivity in relationships also involves empathy. Understanding that everyone has their own struggles and challenges can help you be more compassionate in your interactions. Practicing empathy allows you to respond to others with kindness and patience, fostering stronger bonds and greater resilience when challenges arise.

Life is unpredictable, and sometimes we face personal challenges that seem insurmountable—health issues, loss, financial struggles, or family difficulties. In these times, cultivating positivity can feel like an impossible task, but it's during these moments that positivity is most essential.

In the face of personal struggles, positivity is not about ignoring the pain or pretending everything is okay. It's about finding ways to cope with adversity while maintaining hope for the future. You can start by focusing on small, positive actions: taking a walk in nature, reaching out to a friend for support, or practicing gratitude. Even when life is difficult, these small steps can help you feel more grounded and capable of navigating your challenges.

Gratitude is a powerful tool for maintaining positivity in difficult times. When facing adversity, it's easy to focus on what you've lost or what's going wrong. But practicing gratitude shifts your attention to what you still have and the positive aspects of your life. Whether it's your health, your loved ones, or the simple joys of daily life, gratitude helps you stay connected to what matters most and reminds you that there is always something to be thankful for, even in tough times.

Cultivating positivity isn't a one-time event; it's a habit that you can build over time. The more you practice positive thinking, the more natural it becomes. Start by identifying areas in your life where negativity tends to take root, whether it's self-doubt, fear of failure, or frustration with others. Then, consciously work to shift your perspective in those areas.

As with any habit, the more you practice, the stronger it becomes. By making positivity a daily habit, you'll find that you begin to face challenges with more resilience, optimism, and hope.

Positivity is a transformative force that can help you overcome any obstacle. Whether it's shifting your mindset, supporting those around you, or embracing challenges as opportunities for growth, positivity can create a ripple effect that transforms your life and the lives of those around you. Remember, positivity is not about denying difficulties; it's about responding to them in a way that empowers you to keep moving forward.

By cultivating positivity, you choose to face life with resilience, optimism, and grace. Through consistent practice, you will find that positivity becomes not just a mindset, but a way of life—one that helps you navigate challenges, inspire others, and ultimately create the future you desire.

CHAPTER 8: LEADERSHIP THROUGH TRUST AND EMPATHY

"Leadership is not about being in charge. It's about taking care of those in your charge." — Simon Sinek

True leadership is not about titles or authority; it's about inspiring trust and demonstrating empathy. Leadership, in its most effective form, is a partnership built on mutual respect, understanding, and shared goals. We will explore how trust and empathy are the cornerstones of great leadership and how anyone can embody these qualities, regardless of their role or position in life.

Trust is the bedrock of any successful team, relationship, or organization. Without trust, there can be no true leadership. When people trust you, they are more willing to follow your guidance, collaborate with you, and give their best efforts. Conversely, when trust is absent, productivity falters, communication breaks down, and morale drops.

Trust is not earned overnight; it is cultivated through consistent actions over time. As a leader, whether in a formal position or in your personal life, you must demonstrate integrity, reliability, and authenticity. People need to see that your actions align with your words. If you promise something, follow through. If you say you value honesty, be transparent. Trust grows when people know they can count on you.

This consistency doesn't just apply to big promises—it's also about small, everyday actions. Trust is built when you're present for the people you lead, when you listen to their concerns, and when you respect their time and efforts. By being reliable in your day-to-day actions, you show that you're someone people can rely on, no matter the circumstance.

One of the most powerful ways to build trust is through vulnerability. As a leader, it's easy to put up a front of invulnerability—especially in challenging situations. However, true leaders aren't afraid to show their human side. They share their challenges, admit when they don't have all the answers, and ask for help when needed. Vulnerability invites trust because it shows others that you are real, approachable, and authentic.

In a workplace setting, for example, a leader who admits when they've made a mistake or acknowledges their limits makes it easier for others to do the same. This creates an environment where feedback is welcomed, open dialogue is encouraged, and trust becomes a natural byproduct of these behaviors.

Leaders who inspire trust lead by example. They demonstrate the values they expect from others, and their behavior sets the tone for the entire team. A leader who practices accountability, transparency, and fairness sets a model for others to follow. Whether you're leading a team at work, guiding a family, or mentoring others in your personal life, your actions as a leader will speak louder than your words.

Great leaders understand that they are the role model for their teams. They know that every action they take, every decision they make, will ripple out and influence the actions of those around them. When you lead by example, you make trust a natural part of the culture you're creating.

While trust is essential, empathy is what allows a leader to connect with others on a deeper level. Empathy is the ability to understand and share the feelings of others. It's about putting yourself in someone else's shoes and seeing the world from their perspective. This skill is critical for building relationships, resolving conflicts, and motivating others.

Empathy helps leaders build strong, meaningful relationships. When you genuinely understand and care about the experiences and emotions of others, you create a sense of connection that goes beyond superficial interactions. People want to follow leaders who make them feel seen and heard. Empathy allows you to recognize the individual needs, concerns, and motivations of each person, which in turn enables you to tailor your leadership approach to be more effective.

Consider a manager who takes the time to listen to an employee's struggles or challenges outside of work. By acknowledging their personal circumstances and showing understanding, the leader builds rapport and trust with that individual. This not only strengthens the leader-employee relationship but also fosters loyalty, respect, and a sense of belonging.

Empathy begins with active listening. Listening isn't just about hearing the words someone is saying—it's about truly understanding their message, reading between the lines, and responding in a way that validates their feelings. Active listening is an essential leadership skill that allows you to gain insight into the needs of others and to respond in a way that addresses those needs.

When you practice active listening, you show others that their opinions, concerns, and emotions are important to you. In turn, this fosters an environment of open communication and trust. People are more likely to share their ideas, offer constructive feedback, and collaborate when they feel their voice is heard and valued.

Empathy is especially important in conflict resolution. Conflicts are inevitable, whether in a workplace setting, in family dynamics, or among friends. How a leader handles these conflicts can determine the outcome and impact the future of the relationship. When conflicts arise, an empathetic leader takes the time to understand all perspectives involved and seeks a resolution that addresses everyone's concerns.

When leading through conflict, it's essential to approach the situation with compassion and patience. An empathetic leader doesn't rush to judgment or dismiss people's feelings. Instead, they focus on understanding the underlying issues and helping individuals work through their differences with respect and dignity.

For example, if there's a disagreement between team members, an empathetic leader will take the time to listen to each person's perspective, acknowledge their feelings, and guide the group toward a solution that benefits everyone. Rather than taking sides or imposing a solution, the leader fosters a sense of collaboration and mutual respect, allowing the team to come together and find common ground.

Empathy is also a powerful motivator. When people feel that their leaders understand and care about their personal well-being and professional growth, they are more likely to be motivated to do their best work. Leaders who show empathy are in tune with the needs and aspirations of their team members, and they work to provide the support and encouragement necessary for their success.

An empathetic leader knows how to inspire others by acknowledging their strengths, offering guidance, and providing opportunities for growth. Whether it's giving positive feedback or helping someone overcome a challenge, empathy allows you to motivate others by recognizing their efforts and showing them that you believe in their potential.

Empathy is a key component of emotional intelligence, which is the ability to recognize, understand, and manage emotions—both your own and those of others. Leaders with high emotional intelligence are better equipped to handle the complexities of human relationships and to navigate the challenges of leadership with grace and effectiveness.

Leaders who demonstrate empathy are more in tune with their own emotions and the emotions of those around them. This awareness allows them to respond to situations in a way that fosters positive outcomes, whether it's diffusing tension, building trust, or motivating others. Empathy, therefore, plays a crucial role in emotional intelligence and is a vital skill for effective leadership.

Leadership doesn't always have to come from a position of authority. Even if you don't hold a formal leadership title, you can still lead with trust and empathy. In any group or setting, leadership is about influencing others and guiding them toward a shared goal. You can lead by demonstrating these qualities in your actions, by supporting those around you, and by inspiring others to do the same.

By practicing empathy and building trust in your interactions, you have the power to influence positive change, no matter your role. Whether you're leading a family, a volunteer group, or a team at work, the principles of leadership through trust and empathy remain the same.

Great leadership is not about command and control; it's about leading with trust, empathy, and a genuine desire to help others succeed. Leaders who embody these qualities inspire loyalty, create supportive environments, and guide their teams toward success. Whether you are in a formal leadership position or leading from within, the principles of trust and empathy can elevate your leadership and transform the lives of those you lead.

As you continue your journey toward becoming a more effective and compassionate leader, remember that trust and empathy are not just qualities you can develop—they are a mindset and a way of being. By leading with both of these qualities, you can create an environment where others feel safe, valued, and empowered to achieve their best.

CHAPTER 9: THE JOURNEY TO YOUR BEST FUTURE

"The future belongs to those who believe in the beauty of their dreams." — Eleanor Roosevelt

What does your best future look like? How do you align your actions with your dreams to create a life that brings fulfillment, success, and joy? The journey to your best future begins with a clear vision, a strong sense of purpose, and the determination to take consistent action every day. Now I am going to show you how to define what you truly want from life, breaking down the steps to get there, and remaining focused on your goals despite the obstacles that may come your way.

Before you can begin working toward your best future, it's essential to define what that future looks like. Your vision will be your compass, guiding you through the challenges, the decisions, and the daily routines that shape your life. So, take a moment and ask yourself, "What is my best future? What do I truly want to achieve in life?"

Your best future is deeply personal. It's not necessarily defined by societal expectations or other people's standards, but by what brings you the most happiness, fulfillment, and sense of purpose.

Your vision may include career aspirations, personal growth, relationships, health, or even spiritual fulfillment. To gain clarity about your vision, consider these questions:

- **What do I want to accomplish in the next 5, 10, or 20 years?**
- **How do I want to feel about myself and my life?**
- **What are the most important values and principles I want to live by?**
- **Who do I want to become, and what do I want to contribute to the world?**

Start by reflecting on these questions in a journal or simply sitting quietly with your thoughts. Let your vision unfold naturally, without pressure or limitations. The more you understand about what you truly desire, the more motivated and inspired you will feel to take action toward achieving it.

Once you have a clear vision, it's time to turn that vision into actionable goals. Goals are the steps that take you from where you are today to where you want to be in the future. The process of setting and achieving goals provides direction, helps you track your progress, and builds your confidence as you work toward your ideal future.

When setting your goals, follow these principles to ensure they are clear, attainable, and aligned with your values:

1. Be Specific

A goal that's vague or unclear is much harder to work toward. For example, instead of saying, "I want to be successful," break that down into specific objectives like, "I want to advance in my career by becoming a manager in the next three years" or "I want to start my own business within the next five years."

2. Set Measurable Milestones

Create goals that have measurable milestones so you can track your progress. For instance, if you want to lose weight, a measurable goal would be, "I will lose 10 pounds over the next two months by exercising three times a week and following a healthy eating plan."

3. Make Your Goals Achievable

While it's important to challenge yourself, your goals should still be realistic. Setting impossible or overly ambitious goals can lead to frustration and burnout. Focus on making steady progress by setting goals that stretch you but are also within your reach.

4. Create a Timeline

Giving yourself a timeline for accomplishing your goals creates a sense of urgency and accountability. Instead of saying, "I will get in shape someday," set a concrete timeline: "I will exercise at least three times a week for the next six months."

5. Ensure Alignment with Your Vision

All of your goals should align with your overall vision. If a goal feels disconnected from your true desires, it may not inspire the level of motivation and dedication needed to achieve it. Ensure that your goals are meaningful and will lead you closer to the life you envision for yourself.

The path to your best future is not without its challenges. It's likely that you will encounter obstacles along the way—whether that's a lack of time, unforeseen setbacks, or even self-doubt. The key to overcoming these challenges is to maintain focus, develop resilience, and keep moving forward despite the difficulties.

Here are a few strategies to help you stay focused and push through obstacles:

Shift Your Mindset

Your mindset plays a huge role in how you approach obstacles. When faced with a challenge, avoid seeing it as a barrier or reason to give up. Instead, view it as an opportunity to learn and grow. Adopting a growth mindset allows you to see every setback as a stepping stone to success.

For example, if you fail at something—whether it's a presentation at work or a personal goal—use that experience as feedback rather than a defeat. Ask yourself: "What can I learn from this?" or "How can I adjust my approach next time?"

Stay Consistent, Even When It's Hard

Consistency is one of the most powerful traits you can develop in achieving your best future. Success is built on small, consistent actions over time. Even when motivation wanes, make the commitment to stay consistent in working toward your goals. This will help you keep your momentum and ensure you continue moving forward, even when you don't feel like it.

For example, if your goal is to write a book, committing to writing just 500 words a day, even when you're tired or uninspired, will slowly but surely get you closer to completing it.

Lean into Support

No one achieves success entirely on their own. Having a support network—whether it's family, friends, mentors, or colleagues—can make all the difference in your journey. Seek out people who encourage and challenge you, and who can provide guidance and wisdom when needed.

Don't hesitate to ask for help, whether that means asking for feedback on your progress or simply leaning on someone during tough times. Surrounding yourself with people who uplift you will help you stay motivated and focused on your vision.

Reframe Setbacks as Opportunities

It's easy to get discouraged when things don't go as planned. However, successful individuals understand that setbacks are not permanent. Instead of seeing failure as the end, reframe it as an opportunity for growth. Ask yourself: "What did I learn from this?" or "How can I improve moving forward?"

Reframing setbacks allows you to maintain a positive outlook and turn challenges into catalysts for growth.

Staying Committed to Your Best Future

Building your best future requires dedication, resilience, and self-discipline. It's about taking consistent action, even when it feels difficult, and remaining committed to the vision you've set for yourself. Here are a few additional tips to help you stay on track:

Visualize Your Future

Visualization is a powerful tool for manifesting your best future. Spend time regularly visualizing the life you want to create—whether that's through meditation, journaling, or simply daydreaming. The more you can picture your desired future in vivid detail, the more motivated you will be to take the necessary steps to make it a reality.

Celebrate Small Wins

Don't wait until you've achieved everything to celebrate. Along the way, take time to acknowledge and celebrate the small victories. Whether that's completing a milestone in your career, making progress on a personal project, or simply sticking to a healthy habit, these moments of success will keep you energized and remind you of the progress you've made.

Stay Adaptable

While it's important to have a clear vision and goal, remain flexible in your approach. Life is unpredictable, and circumstances may change. Be willing to adapt and pivot when necessary. Success often requires innovation and a willingness to change course when it benefits your growth and future.

The journey to your best future may not be easy, but it will be worth it. By clarifying your vision, setting meaningful goals, staying focused, and overcoming obstacles with resilience and determination, you can create the life you've always dreamed of. Remember, it's not about the destination, but the journey—the steps you take every day to move closer to your dreams.

The best future is not something that happens to you; it's something you actively create. You have the power to shape your life and make your dreams a reality. Keep your eyes on your vision, take consistent action, and believe in yourself. Your best future is within reach, and it starts with the first step.

CHAPTER 10: BELIEVE AND ACHIEVE

"What you get by achieving your goals is not as important as what you become by achieving your goals." — Zig Ziglar

In life, one of the most important factors that determine success is belief. Belief in yourself, belief in your dreams, and belief that your future holds infinite possibilities. This chapter is dedicated to helping you cultivate that belief—because with belief comes the power to take action, to push through challenges, and to manifest your dreams into reality.

At the heart of every success story is the foundation of self-belief. Whether you want to climb the career ladder, start a business, transform your health, or improve your relationships, it all begins with believing that you are capable of achieving your goals. In this chapter, we will explore how belief fuels success, how you can build unwavering self-confidence, and how to use this belief to make tangible progress toward your best future.

The Power of Belief

Belief is not just a feel-good concept; it is a potent force that shapes the way we think, act, and interact with the world. It's the quiet but unshakeable foundation upon which every major accomplishment rests. Belief affects everything—from the choices we make to the conversations we have with ourselves. The way we think about ourselves and our abilities directly influences the outcome of our lives.

When you truly believe in yourself, you stop limiting yourself with "what-ifs" and "I can't's." You start replacing self-doubt with determination and begin seeing every obstacle as an opportunity to grow. Think about the times you have succeeded. Perhaps it was a challenging project at work, a personal goal you achieved, or even a simple task that seemed overwhelming at first. What got you through those moments? It wasn't just skill—it was belief.

When you believe in your ability to succeed, you approach life with confidence and resilience. When you doubt yourself, you become paralyzed by fear and hesitation, and this prevents you from taking the necessary steps toward success.

The Role of Self-Talk in Building Belief

The words you speak to yourself are far more powerful than you might realize. Self-talk is the inner dialogue that shapes how you see yourself and your capabilities. It can either lift you up or tear you down, depending on what you choose to say. The language of self-doubt—saying things like "I can't," "I'm not good enough," or "I'm not worthy"—creates a negative feedback loop that keeps you stuck. On the other hand, positive self-talk empowers you to push through challenges and pursue your goals with determination.

To start cultivating a stronger belief in yourself, pay attention to your inner dialogue. Are you your own biggest supporter, or your harshest critic? It's easy to be self-critical, but this only leads to feelings of inadequacy. Start replacing self-limiting thoughts with affirmations that empower you. For example:

- Instead of "I'm not good enough," say, "I am capable, and I have the skills to succeed."
- Instead of "This is too difficult," say, "I will break this down into manageable steps and tackle it one at a time."

- Instead of "I'm too afraid to try," say, "I believe in myself, and I am willing to take the first step."

Over time, the more you consciously change your inner dialogue, the more your belief in yourself will grow. You'll stop seeing yourself as an imposter and start recognizing your true worth and potential.

Building Confidence Through Action

Belief without action is mere fantasy. To turn your dreams into reality, you must back up your belief with consistent action. Confidence grows when you take small, intentional steps toward your goals. Each step forward, no matter how small, is a victory that reinforces your belief in your ability to succeed. In the beginning, this may feel uncomfortable or uncertain. But as you begin taking action, your confidence will grow, and your belief will become stronger.

Action is the bridge between dreaming and achieving. For example, if your goal is to write a book, you won't be able to do so without writing. Each day you write—even if it's just for 15 minutes—brings you closer to your goal. The more you write, the more confident you'll feel in your ability to complete the book. The same goes for any goal—whether it's getting fit, growing your business, or learning a new skill. Confidence comes from doing, not just thinking about doing.

One key to making progress is breaking down your goals into smaller, actionable steps. A big goal can feel overwhelming, but when you break it down, each small step feels manageable and attainable. Focus on one task at a time, and don't worry about the end result right away. Celebrate the small wins along the way, and give yourself credit for the progress you're making.

For example, let's say your goal is to lose 30 pounds. Instead of thinking, "I have to lose 30 pounds," focus on smaller milestones.

Break it down into 5-pound increments, and set a goal to lose 5 pounds over the next month. Celebrate when you achieve each milestone, and recognize that every step you take is a victory. This gradual approach helps build momentum and reinforces your belief in your ability to reach the final goal.

Overcoming Doubts and Fear

No matter how confident you become, doubts and fears will still arise from time to time. Fear of failure, fear of success, or fear of judgment from others can hold you back from reaching your full potential. But remember, these fears are simply thoughts—they do not have to control you. It's normal to feel fear, but don't let it paralyze you. Instead, acknowledge the fear and keep moving forward.

The key to overcoming doubt and fear is reframing them. Instead of seeing fear as something to avoid, learn to view it as a signal that you are pushing yourself out of your comfort zone. Fear is often a sign that you are growing and expanding your capabilities. When you feel afraid, remind yourself that the best things in life happen when we step outside of what feels comfortable and familiar.

For example, if you're afraid of public speaking, the fear of failure might stop you from even considering it. But if you reframe that fear as an opportunity to grow, you might find yourself excited about the chance to improve and expand your skill set. Instead of worrying about how you might fail, focus on how you can learn from each experience and become better next time.

One way to overcome doubt is to ask yourself, "What's the worst that could happen?" Often, our fears are exaggerated, and when we break them down, we realize that the consequences are not as catastrophic as we imagined. By shifting your perspective, you can diminish the power fear holds over you and move forward with confidence.

Creating a Plan and Taking Action

Now that you have the belief and the mindset needed to succeed, it's time to create a plan of action. A plan gives structure to your dreams and provides a clear path forward. Without a plan, it's easy to get distracted or lost along the way.

Start by outlining your goals—both short-term and long-term. What do you want to accomplish in the next six months, one year, or five years? Once you have a clear idea of your objectives, break them down into smaller, actionable steps. Create a timeline for achieving these steps and hold yourself accountable to it.

Remember, the key to achieving any goal is consistent effort. Create a daily routine that aligns with your goals. Whether it's setting aside time each day to work toward your career aspirations, focusing on self-care, or investing in your personal development, make sure you are dedicating time to what matters most.

Also, be flexible. Life doesn't always go according to plan, and sometimes you will face unexpected setbacks or changes. When that happens, adjust your plan as needed, but never lose sight of your end goal. Consistent action, even when life throws you curveballs, is what will ultimately lead you to success.

Surrounding Yourself with Believers

Belief is contagious. The people you surround yourself with play a crucial role in your success. If you're constantly surrounded by negativity, self-doubt, and pessimism, it will be much harder to maintain your belief in yourself. But when you surround yourself with people who believe in you, who support your dreams, and who encourage you to take action, you'll feel empowered to keep pushing forward.

Seek out mentors, friends, and colleagues who share your vision or have already achieved what you aspire to do. Let their stories inspire you, and learn from their experiences. Having a strong support system makes it easier to believe in yourself and your goals because you're not doing it alone.

Belief is the fuel that propels you forward, and with it, you can achieve anything you set your mind to. By fostering self-belief, taking consistent action, overcoming fears, and creating a plan, you are positioning yourself to achieve greatness. Your best future is not out of reach—it's within you, waiting to be realized.

Remember, you are capable. You are worthy. You have everything you need to succeed. The only thing standing between where you are now and where you want to be is your willingness to believe in yourself and take action toward your goals.

Your future is waiting for you, and it's time to step into it. Believe in yourself. Achieve your dreams. The best is yet to come.

For more about Winsome Campbell visit her website: www.winsomecampbell.com

> "Believe you can and you're halfway there." — *Theodore Roosevelt*

ABOUT THE AUTHOR

Winsome Campbell

Winsome Campbell is not just an author; she is a beacon of inspiration dedicated to empowering women to transform their lives from the ordinary to the extraordinary. With an exceptional speaking style honed through her years as a former Toastmaster President, Winsome shares her wealth of knowledge and experiences as both a Life Coach and an educator. With over seven years of classroom teaching experience, she embodies a profound passion for teaching that consistently yields positive results in her students and clients alike.

Since 2010, Winsome has penned over 60 books, each a testament to her commitment to personal development and empowerment. Her journey began in the fast-paced world of corporate banking, where she garnered accolades for being the most outstanding in sales. This background laid the foundation for her belief in the power of networking and connection—key elements she incorporates into her coaching practices to help women navigate their careers with confidence and purpose.

Winsome's dedication to uplifting others extends beyond mere mentorship; it is a reflection of her unwavering love for God, which serves as both her message and motivation. She is on a passionate mission to create a community where women can thrive, embracing their unique strengths and stepping boldly into their destinies.

With Winsome Campbell, audiences discover that the path to an empowered life is accessible, attainable, and filled with promise. Her guidance is a powerful catalyst for transformation, inspiring countless individuals to break barriers and elevate their lives through the art of connection and personal growth.

www.ingramcontent.com/pod-product-compliance
Lightning Source LLC
Chambersburg PA
CBHW070412230526
45471CB00006B/2766